Pregnancy Affirmations

— For Labor & Birth —

COLORING BOOK

This Book Belongs To:

_____

Unlimited
MAMA

How To Use This Book

Childbirth can be scary when you don't know what to expect. You could read 100 birth stories and feel prepared; then have a completely different birth experience yourself. Birth is not something we have full control over.

In my experience, one of the best ways to prepare for childbirth is to learn relaxation techniques, such as affirmations.

Follow these steps to get the best results from this affirmations coloring book:

- **Read over the affirmation before coloring it.**

- **While coloring the letters, repeat the previous words as you work.** This process of repeating helps to memorize the affirmations. For example:

  - When coloring the affirmation "I birth with ease", if you are coloring the word "birth", repeat "I birth".
  - Then, as you move on to color the word "with", repeat "I birth with".
  - Moving on to the word "ease", repeat "I birth with ease".

- **Color the pictures.** The act of coloring is a form of art therapy. Art therapy has been shown to help when coping with anxiety, depression, addictions, and trauma. The act of coloring creates a sort of meditative state for some people, that can be beneficial for reducing anxiety during pregnancy.

Visit **www.unlimitedmama.com** for more relaxation techniques to prepare for childbirth.

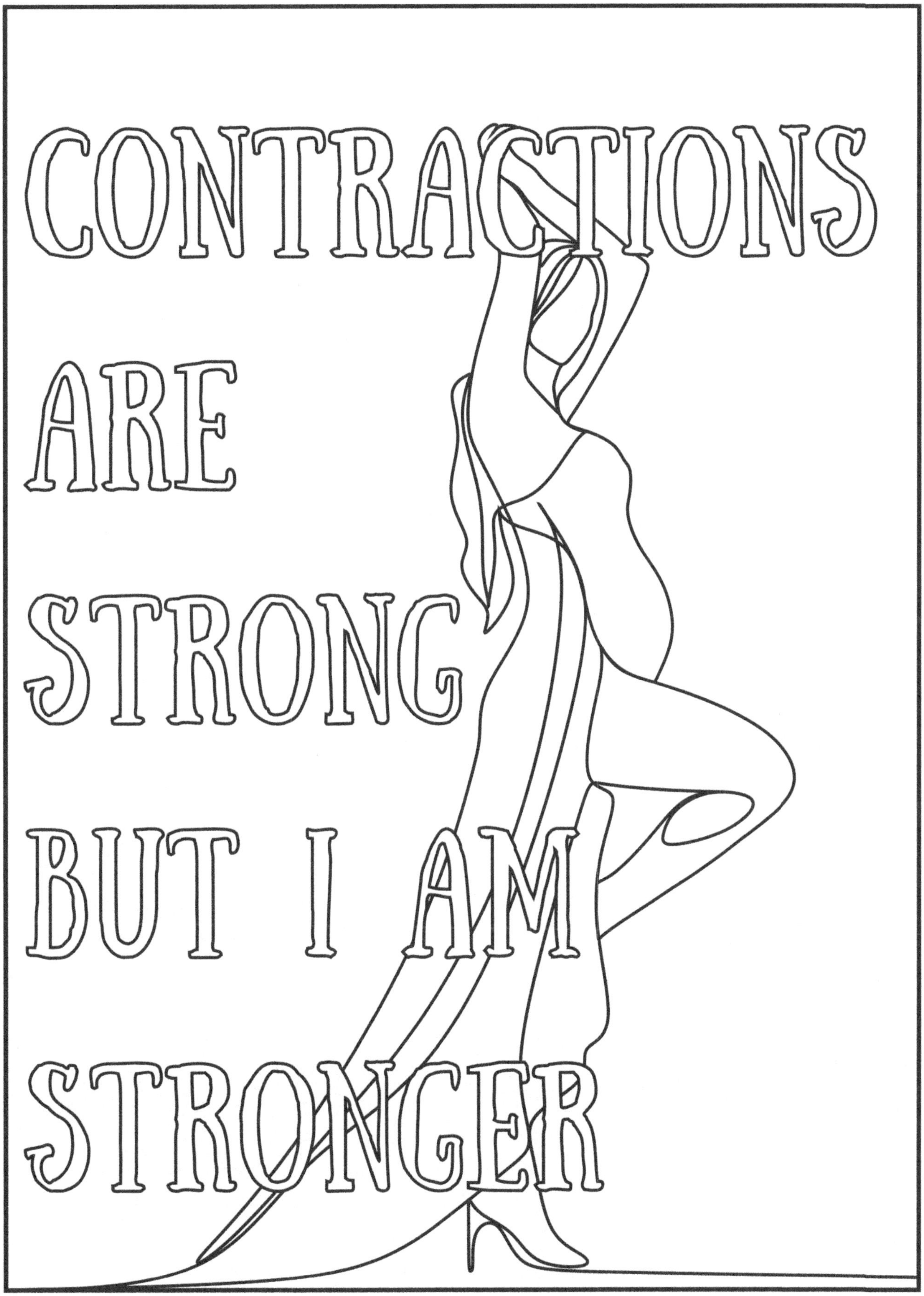
CONTRACTIONS
ARE
STRONG
BUT I AM
STRONGER

I close my eyes
& imagine
my cervix opening

like the doors opening to
my baby's new life.

WOMEN
ALL OVER THE WORLD
birth babies every day.

I CAN DO THIS!

I trust these healthcare professionals to take care of me and my baby

Through every contraction, I TAKE DEEP BREATHS, with closed eyes, open hands, & relaxed muscles.

I am content with any kind of birth my baby needs

I AM GRATEFUL FOR THIS BIRTHING EXPERIENCE

I TRUST THAT MY BODY & MY BABY KNOW WHAT TO DO.

Pain is normal and productive during labor and birth. I close my eyes and take deep breaths.

I AM CONFIDENT
in my body's ability
TO BIRTH THIS BABY

I AM PATIENT IN THIS BIRTHING PROCESS

I LOOSEN EVERY MUSCLE IN MY BODY

head to toe

THROUGH EACH CONTRACTION

MY BODY WAS CREATED TO GIVE BIRTH

BREATHE IN STRENGTH

BREATHE OUT STRESS

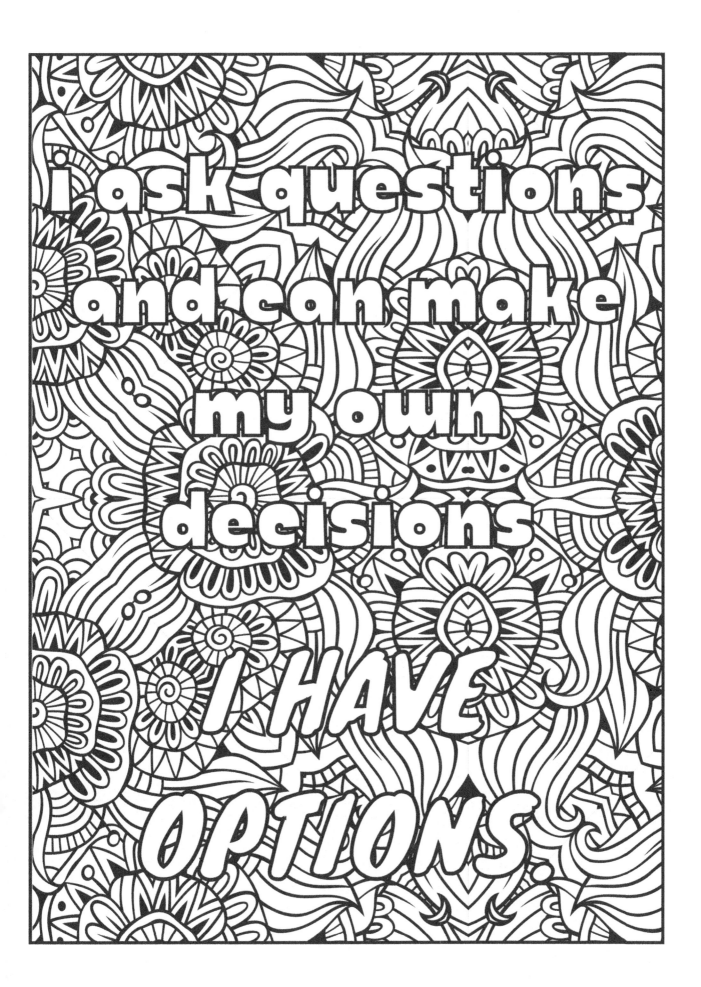

i ask questions and can make my own decisions I HAVE OPTIONS

I FEEL
THE
STRENGTH
OF ALL
WOMEN
WHO HAVE
COME
BEFORE
ME

Made in the USA
Las Vegas, NV
12 April 2024

88586171R00059